Vaughn L. Robinson

Gifts of the Spirit

A book of poems inspired by the Holy Spirit

Copyright @ 2001 by Vaughn L. Robinson

All rights reserved. No part of this book shall be reproduced, stored in a retrieval system, or transmitted by any means without written permission from the author.

Book cover and design by
Carolyn V. Robinson

Gifts of the Spirit

Library of Congress Catalog Number 0001014103

Printed in the United States of America

ISBN: 1-59196-929-8

DEDICATION

This book is dedicated to my wife, Carolyn,

My children,
Vaughn II, Darren, Bobby, Delon, Luseal,
and Vaughndare,

My grandchildren,
Darren, Davaughn, Desiree, Montel, Shontel,
Vaughn III, and Unique

And most of all,
to my loving grandmother, Lovie Robinson,
who shared her love of God with me.

Acknowledgement

I would like to acknowledge

Jesus Christ, first and foremost,
who inspired me through
the Holy Spirit to write these poems.

My wife, Carolyn, for the painstaking hours and
dedication she endured in putting this book together,

My mentor, brother, and friend,
Deacon Otis Sheard

Bishop John H. Sheard for his knowledge and
spiritual leadership, and

My church family,
Greater Mitchell Temple C.O.G.I.C.,
for their continued love and support.

Darren

Oh My Son

Oh my son how could this be,
That God has taken you away from me.

I miss you so
I just can't adjust.
Everything around me
Is in such a mess.

So much love
We used to share,
Now the loss of you
I can hardly bare.

I picture your face,
How it got so bright
When I entered a room
And captured your sight.

I remember how you'd stick out your chest
So proud to introduce me
Now, that was the best.

Your presence is felt still
Day by day.
You didn't really die,
You're just gone away.

The Lord, Salvation

The Lord is my salvation.
He is my guiding light
That fills me up with hope,
And teaches me what's right.

Protects me from the wicked.
No harm will come to me,
Nurturing my soul
So my mind can be set free.

No one shall come before Him,
The master of us all.
With Him we stand in strength,
But without Him we will fall.

My God is really awesome.
I praise Him oh so high.
And cherish His love
Until the day I die.

Advice

Have you ever felt discouraged,
Emotionally depressed.
Did everything you could,
And did it to your best.

With every step forward
You seem to fall back two
Your thoughts begin to wonder
But comes up without a clue

When darkness surrounds you
Life is filled with gloom
This eerie situation
You want to leave but soon

All that I can give you
Is just a little advice
Take it to our Father
Through His son, His name is Christ.

This Day

This day brings me pleasure
And also brings me joy.
I praise my heavenly Father
I've learned to love Him more.

He sees me through my hardship,
And takes away my pain.
He's always there to lean on,
His love will never change.

My God is almighty.
The ruler of this earth.
His spirit is within us,
His body is the church.

In any situation,
Whatever may come about,
I take it to my Father,
Give Him praise and have no doubt.

A Time For Change

A time for change,
The change is with me.
Who am I,
And who do I wish to be?

Time is of the essence
This I see.
I must step up
My spirituality.

My thoughts and actions
Must be with peace and love
Full of the wisdom
From heaven above.

And avoid all things
That make no sense.
While paying particular attention
To my self-centeredness.

From this day forth,
I dedicate my life,
To change for the better,
And the need to sacrifice.

Speaking of the Devil

This is an endless fight,
And I'm on the winning team.
Seductive my opponent,
But he's not the one to esteem.

I am speaking of the devil,
He's as wicked as he can be,
And takes so many forms
When he comes to conquer me.

Suited with an armor
That protects in every way
To know the joy of love,
Have faith in God and what he say.

For God is always watching,
And He gives us what we need
With prayer and belief,
We have planted a fruitful seed.

I mustn't get too cocky,
And forget the devil's lesson.
For as soon as I do,
He will rob me of my blessings.

So each and everyday
I'll give praise and the highest honor.
To God, He's my strength,
And most of all He's my father.

Chosen

Time and time again
I am summoned such a glorious call
Each and every time
I resist and build a wall.

I hear this voice so clearly.
The choice is mine to make.
It's either right or wrong,
He knows if I try to fake.

My desire is of righteousness,
Though the sin temps my flesh.
It's always a constant battle
To be obedient and do what's best.

Written in the scriptures
In my mind these words are frozen.
It states that many are called,
But very few of them are chosen.

My Daughter

This is to my daughter.
My darling baby girl,
Daddy truly loves you
More than anything in this world.

You are so precious to me.
More than your weight in gold,
And when we are together
My life becomes a whole.

I love to see you happy,
And hate to see you sad.
Always keep a smiling,
Do it for your dad.

My love is everlasting.
Always hold it near.
I love you, my darling daughter.
I love you very dear.

Determination

I have determination
Discipline and drive
To unleash all the power
In order to survive.

I live with compelling purpose
To always be my best
And celebrate what I have
To endure and pass all tests.

My only destination
Like a one-way street
Straight forward this direction
I never will retreat.

This journey I am taking
Is not the least bit odd
I'm searching for the wisdom
And the power of my God.

Let Love

Let love remove the shadow,
Melt the chillness of the heart.
Let love be in spirit,
Allowing kindness to play its part.

Let love be the answer
To the many questions asked.
Let love be the solution
To whatever is the task.

Let love erase the doubt,
Replacing it with trust.
Let love do the healing
With its sentimental touch.

Let love break the barriers
Be the wrecking ball of hate.
Let nothing quench the thirst for love.
Let love, let love be fate!

A Gift

On Sunday morning about 12:45
A night I'll always remember.
Stars were bright, twinkling light.
It was the 3rd of December.

I was on my knees giving praise to God,
When I felt the Holy Spirit.
A tingling chill came over me,
The best, nothing else comes near it.

Then picked up my pace a little taste.
Giving thanks saying hallelujah.
To my surprise I spoke some words
In a language and never knew it.

There are many gifts from heaven above,
An honor to receive.
The gift of tongues was granted me,
Glory, glory hallelujah!

My Son, My Heart

I love you my son,
With all my heart.
There is nothing in this world
That could tear us apart.

You're that sacred source,
That let's me know
I will live on in spirit
And continue to grow.

This highest honor
A man could ever achieve,
A son of my likeness
Developed from my seed.

So precious to have
Such a son as you.
I'm so proud to be your father,
And I love you very true.

My Joy, My Peace

There is no greater joy,
Than the peace I have within,
I owe this to my Father,
My Savior and my friend.

He gives to me direction,
A way of living life.
Obeying His instructions,
I avoid temptation and strife.

My God is very gracious,
And merciful yes indeed,
He showers me with blessings,
And fulfills my every need.

I praise my heavenly Father,
From dawn until sunset.
He never leaves me lonely,
Or with feelings of regret.

Praise Pays

I do a lot of work,
Quite a bit is on my knees,
Praising my Lord and Father,
End results I am appeased.

He always lends an ear,
And His love is surely there,
Forgives me for my sins.
This is true He really cares.

As long as I believe in Jesus Christ,
The things he did,
Obey my heavenly Father,
Then I'm sure to have a friend.

Although I call it labor,
I do it everyday.
Giving praise to my Father
And it pays in many ways.

Spreading Love

Judging from my perspective,
The events of everyday,
There is but one solution
Spreading love in every way.

This problem that has consumed us
Affects whatever we do.
It causes plenty of hardship,
In our nation and across seas too.

The amount of all this bitterness
Exchanged from man to man
Could all be resolved by spreading
Love across this land.

I know this is the answer
To the worldwide misery.
Spreading love to all brothers,
Then we can live in harmony.

My Lamp

I serve the Lord with gladness,
I honor Him with song.
Obedient to His statutes,
Avoiding what is wrong.

Having trust in God my Father.
His words a lamp to my feet,
And lights a path before me.
With Him there's no defeat.

I call to you with all my heart,
Answer me O Lord,
Hear my plea and rescue me.
All my faith is yours.

Your righteousness is everlasting,
And your laws are always true.
Direct my steps accordingly,
My life belongs to you.

A Time For Healing

A time for healing
And spiritual forgiving.
A meeting of our souls
A mending of the old.

Forgive….
This thing I've done.
My suffering is not
fun.

This time we've been apart
Brought misery to my heart.

Let these lines begin
The healing and to end
That which I have done
So we can just have fun.

Focus

Reach for your goal,
Whatever that might be.
Stay focused on the plan,
'Till it turns to reality.

Go for that dream.
Move forward to the test,
Although you may stumble,
Stand up and do your best.

All things derive from thought.
The mind's eye of you and me,
Keep your brain in action,
Aroused with curiosity.

There is sure to be obstacles
Standing in your way.
Use them as stepping stones
A path to a brighter day.

Time To Love

Time passes swiftly
Out of man's control.
It keeps right on moving,
Keeps moving right along.

As hours turn to days,
So do days turn into years.
Our youth fades us slowly,
Old age becomes our fear.

We must take advantage
Of every second we're awake.
Love one another, do no harm
For heaven's sake.

It's time to set an example
For the young and me and you.
Loving all our brothers
By all means whatever we do.

Today I Live

Today I live,
And life is great.
I never have to worry
About my fate.

All those problems
That troubled me so,
I've finally realized
How to let them go.

It's only by faith,
That I make this call
And being true to that faith
I can conquer all.

God is good,
All the time.
And I'll be serving my heavenly Father
Because He is divine.

This relationship is okay.
That is why I LIVE today.

A Golden Opportunity

A window of opportunity
Is a moment that will surely pass.
To be aware of that moment,
For some is a lifelong task.

Those who have the privilege
To act when the times arise
Are rewarded with moving forward,
And collecting its worthy prize.

Opportunity is like the seasons,
They come and they go around.
Be fast to harvest its fruits
And realize when it can be found.

This bit of information of importance
For the world to receive
Is a golden opportunity
To be all that we can be.

Word, Love Grows

No worry about the past,
Worry is a waste of time,
Strain for what's ahead,
With patience that are defined.

The true, the pure, the lovely,
Is focus that's a must.
Avoiding negative thinking,
Will help deliver us.

Things that are uncertain.
No confidence in the flesh.
Trust the Lord our savior,
His guidance is the best.

No rush in anything,
But prayer and petition to Christ.
Giving thanks for His presence,
And the entrance into our life.

The plan for the future,
When it comes to setting goals,
More wisdom of God my Father,
His word, gives love and grows.